HOW Video Games ARE MADE

by Noah Leatherland

Minneapolis, Minnesota

Credits

Images are courtesy of Shutterstock.com, unless otherwise stated. COVER & RECURRING – DestinaDesign, BlurryMe, ONYXprj, yudha satia, ST.art, Cuteness here, Dooder, Rolau Elena, Gazoukoo, my.ordinarty. 4–5 – 29september, StockImageFactory.com. 6–7 – Frame Stock Footage, Pixel-Shot. 8–9 – Chaosamran_Studio, MarbellaStudio. 10–12 – deagreez, SeventyFour. 12–13 – Gorodenkoff, DC Studio. 14–15 – Frame Stock Footage, Studio Zero. 16–17 – Gorodenkoff, Bertha Bert. 18–19 – aijiro, Dmytro Sheremeta. 20–21 – Deliris, PrinceOfLove. 22–23 – Frame Stock Footage, DC Studio. 24–25 – Julian Sarmiento, logoboom. 26–27 – l i g h t p o e t, DC Studio. 28–29 – Roman Samborskyi, Frame Stock Footage. 30–31 – Trzykropy.

Bearport Publishing Company Product Development Team

Publisher: Jen Jenson; Director of Product Development: Spencer Brinker; Editorial Director: Allison Juda; Editor: Cole Nelson; Editor: Tiana Tran; Production Editor: Naomi Reich; Art Director: Kim Jones; Designer: Kayla Eggert; Designer: Steve Scheluchin; Production Specialist: Owen Hamlin

Library of Congress Cataloging-in-Publication Data is available at www.loc.gov or upon request from the publisher.

ISBN: 979-8-89577-086-3 (hardcover)
ISBN: 979-8-89577-476-2 (paperback)
ISBN: 979-8-89577-203-4 (ebook)

© 2026 BookLife Publishing
This edition is published by arrangement with BookLife Publishing.

North American adaptations © 2026 Bearport Publishing Company. All rights reserved. No part of this publication may be reproduced in whole or in part, stored in any retrieval system, or transmitted in any form or by any means, electronic, mechanical, photocopying, recording, or otherwise, without written permission from the publisher. Bearport Publishing is a division of FlutterBee Education Group.

For more information, write to Bearport Publishing, 3500 American Blvd W, Suite 150, Bloomington, MN 55431.

Contents

How Things Are Made 4
Ideas and Imagination 6
Concept Art. 8
Building a Game 10
Prototype 12
Animations 14
Motion Capture 16
Voice Acting 18
Sound and Music 20
Testing 22
Promotion 24
Launch 26
Support 28
Your Next Project 30
Glossary 31
Index 32
Read More. 32
Learn More Online 32

How Things Are Made

Do you like making things?

Your favorite books, TV shows, and video games came from the minds of people just like you! It takes a group of talented people to turn a concept into a bestselling video game.

Video games are played on computers, phones, tablets, and **consoles**.

There are many steps to creating these forms of entertainment. How are video games made?

Many video games on consoles are played using controllers.

A video game controller

Ideas and Imagination

Before they can create a video game, **designers** need an idea.

Sometimes, one designer works on all the parts of a game. But usually, a whole team works together to turn an idea into a video game.

There are all sorts of video games. Some games are action-packed and thrilling. Others are calm and relaxing.

Any idea can become a video game. Video game creators just have to figure out how to make it.

Concept Art

Once game designers have an idea, they think about what the game could look like. Artists make concept art to help.

A concept is a rough idea. Concept art shows how something could look. It often shows lots of options.

Some artists draw ideas for characters. Others draw the world the game might take place in.

Concept art helps the whole team understand what they are making.

Many video game artists draw concept art on tablets or computers.

Building a Game

Once creators know what the game will look like, they begin to make it. They start writing the computer code.

Computer code

The code is the most important part of a video game. This is the set of instructions the computer follows to run the game.

A **programmer** writes the code. Rough images and sounds are added to the code.

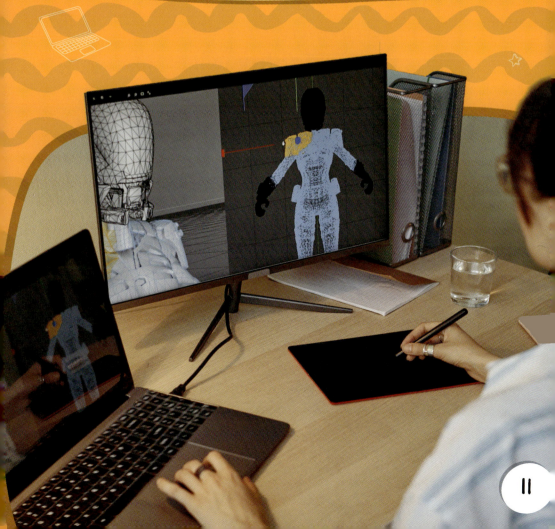

Prototype

All this early work comes together into a prototype. This is the first full version of a game.

A prototype lets creators try the game to give them an idea of what the **gameplay** will be like.

Prototypes often have many problems to solve. But designers learn new things as they make them.

Once they have a prototype that works, the team can start to make the game.

Animations

Most video games are full of moving objects and characters. Characters run around. Trees blow in the wind. Doors open and close.

This is done with animation. Animation is a process that shows pictures one after another very quickly. This makes it look like the pictures are moving.

An animator puts these images together to make the scenes of a game.

Many animators study real animals to recreate an animal's movements in a game.

Motion Capture

To make animations more realistic, animators might use motion capture.

To do motion capture, actors put on special suits. Then, they act out parts of the game. A computer tracks the markings on their suit and **records** their movements.

A motion capture suit

Next, the marks on the suit are matched up to the body parts of game characters. This makes their movements look more real.

Sometimes, motion capture is used with animals, too!

17

Voice Acting

Some games have characters that speak. Their words are recorded by voice actors.

Sometimes, an actor does both the motion capture and the voice acting.

You might also hear a video game character yelp when they get hurt. They may grunt when they jump and climb things. All these noises are recorded by voice actors, too.

Voice actors often record in sound-proof booths to get rid of background noise.

Sound and Music

There are lots of other sounds in video games, too. You might hear a character's footsteps or the sounds of weather.

Sound designers make these noises on computers or by recording the sounds of objects.

Many video games also use music to help make the player feel different emotions. The music could be cheerful, sad, creepy, or exciting.

Composers create the music for video games. Sometimes, they make different music for each level or for each character.

Testing

Once all the parts of a video game are put together, the game needs to be tested.

To do this, teams of people play the game many times to make sure it is working as planned.

These game testers keep track of any problems they find. These problems are called bugs. Testers tell the designers about the bugs so they can change the code to fix them.

Finding and fixing bugs helps future players have a fun time with the game.

Game testers are paid to play and test games!

Promotion

Once a video game is made, it's time to let people know about it through promotion.

Trailers are one way to get people excited about playing a new game. These short videos show off the gameplay with exciting music.

Some video game creators make demos. A demo is a small part of the game that people can play before the full game is released.

Video game **journalists** get to play demos first. If they like a demo, they tell other people how fun the game is.

Launch

Finally, the game is ready to launch. That means it is ready for people to buy and play it.

For online games, players connect to servers to play. Servers are computers that link players together over the internet.

Video game servers

Launch day can be very busy for video game creators. Sometimes, players find bugs in the game that no one saw before.

Players can let the creators know about the bugs. The creators fix them so the game works better for everyone.

Support

Video game creators often keep working on the game even after it has been released.

Sometimes, they add more levels or another piece of the story. These are sent out in updates.

New bugs can happen when updates are sent out. Video game teams need to be ready to fix these problems.

Some creators will work on a game for years after it has launched.

Some virtual reality games use special goggles to make players feel like they are inside the game.

Virtual reality goggles

Your Next Project

There are a lot of people who work together to create video games. Each person has a different set of skills.

What would you do to help create a fun video game? The next big hit could be yours!

Glossary

code instructions a computer follows

consoles machines that video games are played on

designers people who plan and create things

gameplay the parts of a video game that the player controls

journalists people who write news stories

programmers people who write computer codes

records captures pictures or other information into a form that can be used at a later time

updates things that make something more current or modern

Index

actors 16–19
animators 15–16
artists 8–9
bugs 23, 27, 29
characters 9, 14, 17–21
code 10–11, 23
consoles 5
designers 6, 8, 10, 13, 20, 23
journalists 25
updates 28–29

Read More

Bolte, Mari. *Super Surprising Trivia About Video Games (Super Surprising Trivia You Can't Resist).* North Mankato, MN: Capstone Press, 2024.

Minyard, J.G. *Gaming Careers (Jobs on the Edge).* Minneapolis: Bearport Publishing Company, 2025.

Learn More Online

1. Go to **FactSurfer.com** or scan the QR code below.
2. Enter **"Video Games"** into the search box.
3. Click on the cover of this book to see a list of websites.